PLAYGROUND KINDNESS

Miranda Kelly

CRABTREE
PUBLISHING COMPANY
WWW.CRABTREEBOOKS.COM

Our parents teach us **manners.**

They teach us to be helpful and kind.

Good manners help us get along with others.

Use your manners
on the playground.

Take **turns** and be fair.

Do your part to keep the playground clean.

Be sure to **share**.

Look out for each other.

Be a **good** sport.

Good game!

Practice playground kindness every day.

Glossary

good sport (GOOD SPORT): A good sport is someone who uses good manners even when they lose.

manners (MAN-urz): When you use good manners, you are acting polite and kind.

share (SHAIR): When you share, you are using something with someone else.

turns (TURNZ): Turns are chances to do something.

Index

School-to-Home Support for Caregivers and Teachers

Crabtree Seedlings books help children grow by letting them practice reading. Here are a few guiding questions to help the reader with building his or her comprehension skills. Possible answers are included.

Before Reading

- What do I think this book is about? I think this book is about being kind to others. It is about how to get along with others on a playground.

- What do I want to learn about this topic? I want to learn about different ways to be kind to others.

During Reading

- I wonder why... I wonder why the children on pages 16 and 17 are sad.

- What have I learned so far? I have learned that some ways to be kind are to share, take turns, and use manners.

After Reading

- What details did I learn about this topic? I learned that good manners teach us how to be helpful and kind. They help us get along with others.

- Read the book again and look for the vocabulary words. I see the word **_turns_** on page 11 and the word **_share_** on page 14. The other vocabulary words are found on pages 22 and 23.

Library and Archives Canada Cataloging-in-Publication Data

Title: Playground kindness / by Miranda Kelly.
Names: Kelly, Miranda, 1990- author.
Description: Series statement: In my community |
"A Crabtree seedlings book". | Includes index.
Identifiers: Canadiana 20200388150 |
  ISBN 9781427129598 (hardcover) |
  ISBN 9781427129697 (softcover)
Subjects: LCSH: Kindness—Juvenile literature. |
LCSH: Courtesy—Juvenile literature.
Classification: LCC BJ1533.K5 K45 2021 | DDC j177/.7—dc23

Library of Congress Cataloging-in-Publication Data

Names: Kelly, Miranda, 1990- author.
Title: Playground kindness / by Miranda Kelly.
Description: New York, NY : Crabtree Publishing, 2021. | Series: In my community, a Crabtree seedlings book | Includes index.
Identifiers: LCCN 2020050788 |
  ISBN 9781427129598 (hardcover) |
  ISBN 9781427129697 (paperback)
Subjects: LCSH: Playgrounds--Social aspects--Juvenile literature. | Kindness--Juvenile literature. | Etiquette for children and teenagers--Juvenile literature. Classification: LCC GV423 .K45 2021 | DDC 790.06/8--dc23 LC record available at https://lccn.loc.gov/2020050788

Crabtree Publishing Company

www.crabtreebooks.com   1-800-387-7650

e-book ISBN 978-1-947632-82-0
Print book version produced jointly with Crabtree Publishing Company NY, USA

Written by Miranda Kelly
Production coordinator and Prepress technician: Amy Salter
Print coordinator: Katherine Berti

Printed in the U.S.A./012021/CG20201112

Photo credits: Pages 2-3 © istock.com/KatarzynaBialasiewicz, page 4 © istock.com /3sbworld, page 5 © istock.com /monkeybusinessimages, pages 6-7 © istock.com/ bowdenimages, page 9 © g istock.com /pointstudio, page 10 © istock.com /monkeybusinessimages, page 12 © istock.com/joebelanger, pages 14-15 © istock.com / Rawpixel, shutterstock.com/antoniodiaz, page 16 © 589088442, page 17 © Ljupco, page 19 © Wavebreakmedia, pages 20-21 © dolgachov
All photos from istockphoto.com except: Cover and page 12-13 © Rawpixel.com, both from Shutterstock.com

Published in Canada	Published in the United States	Published in the United Kingdom	Published in Australia
Crabtree Publishing	Crabtree Publishing	Crabtree Publishing	Crabtree Publishing
616 Welland Ave.	347 Fifth Ave	Maritime House	Unit 3 – 5
St. Catharines, ON	Suite 1402-145	Basin Road North, Hove	Currumbin Court
L2M 5V6	New York, NY 10016	BN41 1WR	Capalaba QLD 4157